Internal Voice

Seleste G. Swayzer, M.A.

BookLeaf Publishing

Presentation by *BookLeaf Publishing*

Web: www.bookleafpub.com

E-mail: info@bookleafpub.com

ISBN: 9789357617758

First edition 2022

*To anyone who has ever doubted themselves,
believe in yourself enough to follow your heart.*

ACKNOWLEDGEMENT

Above all, I would like to acknowledge my Higher Power, God. Thank You for guiding my steps on my journey.

I want to thank the community of family and friends who support me. I honor you for every word of encouragement that you have uttered to me personally or professionally throughout the years. My interactions with you all keep me motivated to live life on my terms. I am grateful to experience family, friends, and colleagues like you.

"Last, but not least, I want to thank me. I want to thank me for believing in me. I want to thank me for doing all this hard work." -Snoop Dogg

PREFACE

Since about 12 years of age, I've invested energy into pursuing hobbies that piqued my curiosity. For example, I have taken art & photography classes, cooking tutorials, studied two instruments, sang in choirs, played recreational basketball, ran track & field, attempted adult swimming lessons, and participated in yoga instructor training. Similarly, writing has been a lingering pastime of mine as well. I enrolled in a Creative Writing course during my senior year of college, because I figured it would be an enjoyable way to improve my writing skills. However, immediately after graduating with my Bachelor's Degree in Sociology in May 2011, I was confronted with the harsh reality of attaining a "real job" and paying bills. Years later, when I began working with adolescents in public schools, my passion for writing reemerged.

In my professional role as a school psychologist, students often approach me with challenges. They usually do not want a solution or advice, though. They want someone to listen to them, to understand their point of view. They yearn to be validated. I frequently reflect on having those same feelings as a young person. At times, the residual feelings of being ignored or invisible resurface for me as an adult. They were exacerbated during the lockdown period of the Covid-19 pandemic, so I kept journals to cope with those tangled emotions. The journal entries consisted of an array of motivational quotes, spiritual notes, thoughts of gratitude, and poems.

When the opportunity to write a book of poetry presented itself to me in the form of an Instagram challenge, I obsessively researched the publishing company, then I procrastinated. I ruminated over the chance to actualize a goal from my "mental vision board" for several months. I let my fear of the unknown paralyze me into inaction. Luckily, the publishing company engages in writing challenges several times a year. I eventually motivated myself into taking a chance and trying something new, yet again. As you read through this book, you will glimpse into how my internal voice perceives the world. May you be inspired to release your unique inner voice.

I Write...

I write to uplift my inner voice.
For the chance to be recognized
By someone, anyone who understands
The depth of my potential.
I ponder the notion of power attained
From an external source.
There is strength in sharing my story
Despite no one comprehending it.
Without regret, I affirm my prominence.
My voice ascends with each spoken word.

Hibernation

Like a grizzly, I've been sleeping
For months on end.
The frosty chill has come and gone.
Trying to awaken, find my slumbered zeal.
I continue to snooze on life.
Suffocating from the weight of stagnation.
How do I crawl from this den of darkness,
To the spiritual abundance that awaits.

Freedom

Reminisce on the sensation
Where there is excitement and joy.
Cherish it. Embrace the thrill.

I seek freedom
In every sense of the word.
Untethered. Boundless. Liberated.

In pursuit of autonomy to do
whatever, whenever, and however
I choose to do it.

Confession of an Introvert

Presumed socially inept.
I may be quiet, but I am not silent.
Intuition advises my vibrational reciprocity.
Vulnerability in its generous expression
Demands a peaceful landing zone.

Fondness to those who have endured
The lull of a stalled transaction.
Showing genuine consideration for the
Character deep within.

Daily Affirmation

5

I am bold.
I am brilliant.
I am beautiful.

Hope

I seek what eludes me, ever so gently.
The glimmer I once held
With clenched fists
Has slipped from my grasp.

I search for the smallest semblance
Of certainty.
Even a sliver of moonlight would shift
The lowest tides.

Change my misguided conception.
Signifying the seeds I have sown,
May perhaps reap overwhelming hope.

Sunrise

Gazing at rainbow sherbet skies
Preoccupied with endless possibilities.
What is to come of my future?
Where will this day take me,
In the moments ahead?
Not to overwhelm my heart and mind.
Stop! Listen to the birds chirp, "Good morning."
Trust the day will unfold with majestic beauty.
A glorious symbol,
The sunrise.

The Dreamer

My eyes are wide open,
Yet, I am dreaming
Of a better life.

Inundated attainment.
Oriented intentionality.
Being more than I am.

Fierce beliefs,
Dwelling in my dreams.
An alternate reality,
Abounding with transformation.

Public Speaking

Heart palpitations. Shallow Breathing.
Trembling voice. Shaky palms.
Lava barreling through my veins.
Reeky condensation, dripping down
A furrowed brow.

The thought train has derailed.
Remnants of nonsense scattered.
I can't remember what to say.
Why do I feel this way?
No other alternative than,
Anxiety.

Take a deep breath.
Regain composure.
This too shall pass.

Perspective

How I wish I could observe the
World through your eyes.
Glance through your lens.
Maybe I could empathize
With your sense of wonderment,
Your struggle, your elation.
Whether near-sighted or far,
The view is rare.

I desire to take a peek.
Not with my eyes, but with my ears.
As I listen to the untold treasures
Of your mind.
Oh, I can not wait to take a ride,
To a new world,
So divine.

Purpose

Beyond one calling, one destiny.
Exceeding a 9 to 5 job,
Surpass my predesignated role.
My life's work is to be present in the now.
Where I am living out loud.
Screaming and shouting.
I know my why, my purpose is HERE.
(Presence in the moment)

3.1 Miles (5K)

On your mark,
Get set...

Proceeding my launch,
I evoke memories of my incentive at
The starting line.
My preliminary exhilaration,
When I registered for the race.
The buckets of sweat and tears,
In the weeks of training.

A compassionate reminder to run
At my own pace.
No matter how many sprinters dash by,
Nor the intensity of stinging body aches,
Nor the distance to the finish line,
I'm in this race until the end.

Sensitivity

"You're too sensitive!"
Words hurled at me like a
Ball I should dodge.
I stand tall, in acceptance
Of my Sensitive nature.

Awareness of subtle changes,
Other's feelings and easily emotive.
It's my superpower.
I cry when I'm hurt,
Shriek with joy,
Boil in anger.
I feel it all, ever so intensely.

To lower my head in shame from
Accusations, "You're too this, You're too that."
It will not be.
I welcome the goodness inside.
I will forever reply,

Yes! I am sensitive!

Destination

Location. Aim. Haven. End of the line.
Birth of a subsequent journey.

Love

Incessantly captivated
By one individual.
Devoted through ebbs and flows.
Longing for his familiarity.
Conversely, one truth remains.
Every person will inevitably change.
So, I fall for his essence, his heart.
The true composition of his being.
Reverence for his soul.

Shine

Radiance surrounds you.
Your aura, your glow.
The beam is blinding.
It illuminates the world.
Let your light shine bright.

Gratitude

I am grateful for what has passed.
I am grateful for what is here.
I am grateful for all that is to come.

October 21

Today, I reset
Begin anew.
Aiming to be distinctive,
Focus on the positive.
Attract sublime circumstances.
Faith that what is meant to be,
Cannot bypass me.